THE
CLASSIC
ROCKIES

A great lone land
Vast and sublime
Jutting skywards
The Canadian Rockies

THE
CLASSIC
ROCKIES

TEXT AND PHOTOGRAPHS BY GEORGE BRYBYCIN

GB PUBLISHING

CALGARY, ALBERTA

CONTENTS

Preface

Writing the introduction for this 39th book is not easy because whatever could be said about the Rockies has been said in previous publications. However, the author has a strong propensity to come up with new ideas and different angles to portray the subject.

This volume features the Rockies in order of geographical regions: starting south at the U.S. border in small, but lovely, Waterton Park; then continuing north to a large semi-protected region known as Kananaskis Country – having within its boundaries Provincial Parks and Wilderness Parks. Further north, a crown jewel of the Rockies, a World Heritage Site, is spectacular Banff National Park, Alberta. Over into British Columbia to the west is the verdant and pristine Kootenay National Park, known for its numerous and diverse wildlife. Still on the British Columbia side, north of Kootenay, is Yoho National Park, small in area, but huge in physical features. Yoho houses several large waterfalls, lakes, icefields and glaciers, as well as a number of high and challenging mountains. Further north of Banff Park sprawls the largest and wildest of all the Rocky Mountain National Parks, another renowned World Heritage Site – Jasper National Park, Alberta, where you will find all that a great National Park ought to offer.

No portrait of the Rockies would be complete without majestic Mount Robson, the monarch of the Rockies. The final chapter of this book features fascinating Mount Robson Provincial Park, British Columbia.

It is the author's intention to present the Rockies in their natural, pristine state, just as his previous publications have done, so please do not expect to see many man-made creations. The reason is simple – humans may try to improve on nature, to better it somehow, but to no avail. Nature is so meticulously superior – perfect - that we shall not attempt to tamper with her. Leave nature be and the wilderness will remain as wild and fascinating as ever. You will notice more photos featuring gentler forms of the Rockies such as meadows, lakes, rivers and green areas, in contrast to some of the author's previous books which have featured the stark beauty of high vistas and rugged lofty peaks. A high altitude landscape consists of a jagged, stark, and brooding world where only a tumbling avalanche, wind, or sharp whistle of a Marmot or Pika, break the silence. There are several photos of this lofty world included in order to show what the author was witnessing on the high silvery ridges.

Some wildlife images are also presented with just a word of caution to tourists from faraway places who may love to photograph Grizzly Bears with a little pocket cameras. Be aware that every year people are hurt or killed when they approach wild animals too closely. All Bears, Cougars, Moose and Elk and, in particular, females with their young, are dangerous. Even small game, when cornered or feeling threatened, can be very efficient in defending themselves. Remember to stay at least 50 metres from large animals and remain in your car when a Bear is in the vicinity.

When venturing into back country for a long hike or overnight camping trip, be sure to familiarize yourself with local regulations, conditions and hazards. Talk to Parks Canada Information personnel, equip yourself well so you can survive an extra day in case you become lost or have an accident. It is not just an old cliché that the wilderness is hazardous and dangerous; it is a reality and the truth. Be diligent, play it smart and safe (carry some Bear spray) and enjoy outstanding unforgettable wilderness jaunts in the fascinating Canadian Rockies.

Hopefully the photos featured in this volume will guide you into many interesting, marvelous places in the Canadian Rockies.

Introduction

A good part of western North America is blessed with impressive and diverse mountains stretching from the bold flat Prairies on the east to the jagged Pacific Coast to the west. Several separate distinct mountains are located in western parts, while the Rockies noted for their aloofness and grandeur occupy the eastern flanks bordering the Prairies. Contrary to some belief, the Rockies do not reach the Pacific coast, but are quite a narrow range (circa 80-100 km wide). The Canadian Rockies stretch from the U.S. border to the Yukon border where the Liard River defines their northern perimeter.

On the site of a tropical sea, millions of years ago, violent volcanic activity uplifted solidified sediments from the sea bottom and pushed them up and eastward. Some strata, even today, indicate fossils of tropical fish, invertebrates and plants, high up on the mountains. (Picking fossils is against the law and violators are prosecuted). One hundred million years ago a major tectonic turmoil continued pushing strata ever higher up, which folded and cracked violently, creating extremely rugged environments. Eons of climatic changes, erosions, earthquakes – nature at work – smoothed down the rugged mountains somewhat. As recently as 10,000 years ago, cyclical cooling occurred. Wisconsin Glaciation pushed south into what is now the United States. Today we experience the more-man-than-nature-made global warming trend, which is rapidly melting ice all over the world, causing the rise of the oceans at alarming rates. If humans continue growing in numbers, producing, consuming and creating pollution (the cause of all environmental problems), the consequences will be irreversible and totally unpredictable (one problem leads to more problems). Future generations may see only old pictures of the gorgeous emerald-green glacial lakes and rivers we enjoy today. The Rockies are on average 2600 to 3100 metres high. There are around 500 peaks exceeding 3000 metres. The monarch of them all is Mt. Robson (3954m), second is Mt. Columbia (3747m), then Twin North (3683m), Clemenceau (3658m), Alberta (3619m), Assiniboine (3618m), Forbes (3612m), Twins Tower (3596m), Goodsir South (3562m), Twin South (3558m), to name ten of the highest.

Most mountains of the Rockies are of limestone, very carved and shaped by glaciation during various times. Fast retreating glaciers now expose smooth, polished solid rock – a history written in the rock. Mountains are weather makers and keepers, creating their own microclimate. Global wind circulation is of west-east pattern. Warm moist Pacific air drifts eastward unobstructed until it reaches the lofty Rockies, which are as high as the altitude clouds travel. There are heavy rains and snowfalls on the west side of the Continental Divide while the leeward side receives much less moisture, only a fraction of which reaches the ever-thirsty Prairies.

Life in the Rockies is defined by altitude, latitude and seasons. Three basic climatic zones are quite distinctive:

The first, low valleys full of diverse flora and fauna where life prospers or exists year round. The large forests are home to mammals and predators. Nesting birds and fish are plentiful and winter is bearable.

The second zone reaches the 2100 to 2400 metre level and is more seasonal than permanent. Here at the tree line and higher, gorgeous flowery meadows provide a summer paradise for many species, large and small, but this fine "summer resort" is open only for less than four months as winter reigns here for seven to eight months.

Third is the Alpine or Arctic zone above 2400 metres. Life here is hard and quite limited. Only very few hardy dwellers like Pika, Squirrels, and Weasel, spend a short "summer" here, then move to the second or first zone for the endless winter which at higher elevations lasts ten months, and on mountains over 3400 metres is permanent. This is a harsh and inhospitable world, yet.....some critters called 'mountain climbers' camp here on snow or ice and pretend that they enjoy it!

People of the Rockies? Yes, there is a small permanent population of hardy folks who do not mind one bit the harsh winters and dangers of this vast and sublime world where rocky giants jut skywards. Come summer, millions of vacationers flock to the mountains for holidays or stay longer for physical and spiritual renewal. There is a lot to do and see here. Sightseeing is the main activity; the more adventurous and energetic types hike deeper into the wilderness. Those yet more determined scramble or climb lofty summits to 'get high on the Rockies'.

There are plenty of water sports to enjoy, fishing, horseback riding or wilderness camping, but bear in mind the Bears. Artists find incredible scenery to paint or photograph, musicians are inspired to compose cantatas and sonatas, just listening to the mountain breezes. When winter comes, one may assume this great lone white land goes to sleep? Not so – life buzzes on, a bit harsher for wildlife, but most endure and survive. Only the clever Bear, Marmot and a few others, hibernate in cozy warm dens to escape the worst of winter.

The rigors of winter do not deter one species, however, who migrate here by the thousands and crowd the white slopes any day of the winter. These are the skiers. The Rockies are blessed with generous snowfalls – mostly powder – and several world-class ski resorts are to be found here. Today the Rockies are accessible by excellent highways, by train and by air. World-class hotels, restaurants and services, guarantee memorable vacations. The Rockies are still quite pristine, green and beautiful, for one reason only -most of them are protected by the National Parks System along the Continental Divide. It all started back in 1885 when wise people created Banff National Park, the first in Canada, to protect the sulphur hot springs which were seen as the future site of a mountain resort. The following year, Yoho National Park was created, Waterton followed in 1895, Jasper in 1907, and Kootenay in 1920.

Together with several Provincial Parks and Wilderness Parks, most of the Rockies are to some degree protected, but unfortunately not all is well in paradise. There is a gap between Waterton and Kananaskis, well over 100 kilometres long, completely unprotected, free for all, where logging, mining, development, and hunting goes on destroying the wilderness. Provincial Parks and so-called Wilderness Parks do not provide adequate protection from inconsiderate people who poach and use off-road vehicles just for kicks (destroying the wilderness). More and more development continues adjacent to National Parks. Pollution, noise, and increasing traffic, disrupt wildlife and contradict the very purpose of National Parks. What should be mandatory is a 10 kilometre buffer zone around each Park, where no major development, logging or hunting, would be permitted. Canada, being a large country, could readily protect all natural areas of significant value yet less than three percent of the country's landmass is protected. Many environmentally-concerned countries aim at protecting 10% of their land by building verdant industries – eco-tourism, instead of smoky poison-inducing heavy industries. Closing this Waterton-Kananaskis gap, creating a large new Tornado National Park from Highway 3 north to Kananaskis and enlarging Waterton Park north to Highway 3, is urgently needed now. This action would protect the entire backbone of the Rockies.

A few words needs to be said about the purpose of National Parks and what the rules concerning them are. The original National Park Act of 1930 describes the purpose of a Park in this way: *"The National Parks are hereby dedicated to the people of Canada for their benefit, education and enjoyment, subject to this Act and the regulations and the National Parks shall be maintained and made use of so as to leave them unimpaired for the enjoyment of future generations"* (short excerpt). The Parks were meant for public possession, which means that we all could enjoy them. The Act like many legal documents is too general, having many loopholes. Over time several amendments to the Act were implemented, including more loopholes, giving more authority to local administrators in the making of major decisions. This resulted in changes in the direction in which Parks are going and eroded the original concept of a National Park. The Act says, "leave them unimpaired" meaning pristine, natural, undisturbed. Yet, parts of some Parks are built up, noisy, and polluted. Rivers and lakes contain water unfit to drink. Hundreds of animals are killed each year by growing traffic. Some species of animals and plants are near extinction in our "protected" National Parks. Nobody has a clear idea of how to handle increasing numbers of visitors. A quota system may be a coming solution; in the meantime, more public education and awareness may be in order.

It is difficult to determine how many people display total ignorance about what National Parks are for, but the numbers are high. Just sit in your car on a large parking lot by a lake and you will see in the matter of one hour 10 to 15 people breaking Park rules: throwing garbage, picking flowers, trampling grass, feeding wildlife, walking off trail, letting dogs run unleashed, throwing rocks into the lake, etc. These are the same people who trample on the grass in our City parks, destroying them as soon as the City repairs the damage (your tax dollars).

God forbid, do not try to reprimand them – you will certainly be told loud and clear where to go – the attitude is always the same: "I do as I please!" The only way to educate arrogant, ignorant folks is to hand them a $100 fine for any infractions. Why don't wardens and police enforce the law? It would fill their coffers full of money which could be used to maintain Parks and at the same time it would educate the inconsiderate.

When in the National Parks or any wild lands, walk on the trails only, do not move or take anything. Just take pictures and leave only light footprints – that means, leave the place as is, unimpaired forever.

A large complex of preserved land like the five Rocky Mountain National Parks provides Canada and the world with a vast amount of fresh air and a healthy lifestyle we all can enjoy. The more conserved land, the better. Have you ever considered bequeathing your land to the Nature Conservancy of Canada? This noble organization will conserve your land so it will never see the bulldozer of a developer. Give them a call soon.

We conclude this writing with a quote from "Alpine Meadows" by the author. "If there is a Kingdom of beauty, tranquility and inspiration, it must be high above the tree line in the glorious mountain meadows of the Canadian Rockies – a realm of wild natural beauty and peace."

Waterton Lakes National Park

This very scenic and idyllic Park created in 1895, only ten years after Banff Park, was named after a famous 18th century English naturalist, Charles Waterton. Comparatively small, this 505 km² Park protects some very unique ecology – a transition zone from the Prairie grasslands to the Rocky Mountains with no foothills in between. The east perimeter of the Park is home to a modest herd of Buffalo confined to a small paddock. In the spring when the land is moist, an incredible variety of plants and flowers carpet the paddock, to the delight of the Buffalo. Crocus and Glacier Lily dominate the scene in May.

In the eastern parts of the Park sprawl great flat plains where vegetation is abundant. Come winter, hundreds of ungulates migrate here as warm Chinook winds melt snow quickly, making foraging easy. This winter range may support as many as 1500 Elk, not to mention other ungulates. In the central area of the Park by the Upper Lake is cradled the picturesque little town of Waterton, providing all the essential services for tourism.

Two scenic roads access the western parts of the Park. Cameron Lake road offers great scenery and a few hiking trails: Lineham Lake trail; renowned Tamarack Trail along Rowe Creek leading to the Park's remote northwestern part; Akamina Trail which crosses into the B.C. Rockies and Cameron Lake area offers a trail to Summit and Carthew Lakes continuing east to Waterton. The Canadian portion of Cameron Lake is three kilometres long and after crossing the Montana border the Lake's southern perimeter is set against the high wall of the Continental Divide. Here on the lush green avalanche slopes Grizzly Bears spend the summer and the mighty Moose frequent the area as well. Northeast of town Red Rock Canyon road meanders westward along Blakiston Creek and features Crandell campsite. There is also a trail along Bauerman and Blakiston Creeks, both connecting to the north end of Tamarack Trail. Red Rock Canyon exposes interesting strata of colourful rock formations and is a favourite spot for Mountain Sheep.

Upper, Middle and Lower Waterton Lakes are large bodies of water which provide magnificent scenery and all manner of water sports. The southeastern portion of the Park is isolated by these Lakes but contains a prime attraction – Cript Lake trail. The only way to get there is by shuttle boat. The trail features passage through a tunnel and several waterfalls.

The Park's highest mountain is Mount Blakiston (2910m) named for Thomas Blakiston, ornithologist of the Palliser Expedition of 1858-60. The Park is known for invigorating breezes year round which in winter cause a gale-strength Chinook to thaw snow quickly, making it easier for wildlife that winter here. In the second half of June, Waterton hosts the Wildflower Festival – a not-to-be-missed spectacle as the Park is home to nearly 900 species of plants. In July a unique 'show' takes place – Waterton's showiest flower – Bear Grass – can be admired. This creamy-white plant can reach one meter in height and grows here at its northern limits.

Bird watchers will also be delighted as more than 250 bird species visit the Park in the summertime. This lovely cozy Park has only one major annoying problem and it is that the Park is much too small. Urgently it should be enlarged north to highway 3 before developers' bulldozers overrun the area.

Right: Nowhere in the Canadian Rockies except in Waterton Lakes National Park can Bear Grass (Xerophyllum tenax) be found and admired. A perennial showy plant reaching over one metre in height, is creamy-white in colour and prefers dry, sunny slopes where it forms dense stands. Perennial it may be, but it displays a cyclical characteristic: one year Bear Grass is plentiful, next year hardly any.

*Above: O*n the way to Cameron Lake, almost hidden, the picturesque Cascades tumble gently down on Cameron Creek. *The Creek originates at Cameron Lake and meanders for 16 kilometres to reach the town of Waterton. Here, just before the Creek reaches Upper Waterton Lake, water tumbles over old exposed strata forming a well known tourist site – Cameron Falls (left). The best time for viewing the Falls is June when snow in the mountains melts rapidly causing the Falls to roar.*

Above: When in Waterton a short hike to the Bear Hump on Mt. Crandell is a must. The trail starts at the Information Centre and the little effort the hike takes is well worth it. You will see Upper Waterton Lake (photo) and the great mountains along the Lake. To the left you will see the Middle and Lower Lakes and the town's landmark – the quaint old hotel on the hill. Below is bustling downtown Waterton and the marina as Vimy Peak looks on (left).

Above: O*wing to strong warm winds Waterton is known to be dry but not in early summer. At the Bison Paddock a member of a small herd of Plains Bison (Bison bison) enjoys the lush green flowery pasture. These fascinating resilient animals are more or less extinct in the wild. A few herds survive in some National Parks, wildlife reserves and private ranches.*

Left: A *dry and windy day along Red Rock Canyon Road. This 25-kilometre long valley along Blakiston Creek provides outstanding scenery and wildlife viewing opportunities. In autumn when berries are plentiful, the valley is home to several Bears, Black and Grizzly. Other game to view here are Elk, Deer, Sheep, Goat and, of course, carnivores looking for their next meal.*

A short three-kilometer hike along a well-graded trail leads to spectacular Bertha Falls. The water emanates from Bertha Lake, another three kilometers up a rather steep trail. Visit the Falls in June when the water level is up owing to rapid snow melt at higher elevations. During the first half of July the Bear Grass looks delightful.

Bertha Lake and its surroundings are nothing short of a virtual paradise. A rewarding six kilometer hike offers many interesting features alongside this two-kilometer long Lake. Completely surrounded by steep mountains: Mt. Richards, Mt. Alderson and Bertha Peak, the Lake creates its own microclimate where vegetation thrives and the variety and profusion of flowers is overwhelming.

Above: As described on page 15, Red Rock Canyon Road features many attractive sights: one of them a large stand of poplar. Although it is October 10, and the trees are leafless, the morning light creates a warm ambience to the scene. Ruby Ridge at centre, the highest in the Park and snowy Mt. Blakiston (2910m) add an alpine touch.

Left: As the name implies 'red rock' appears on the lower slopes of Mt. Galwey (2348m). Gentle lower slopes give way to a steep and challenging summit. In early July the author and dozens of visitors viewed a mama Grizzly and two cubs grazing. From above the rolling hills and humps, two people with two small children were approaching, unaware of the danger. The horrified crowd started shouting, waving their arms and honking horns, but the hikers being over one kilometer away thought everyone was greeting them and kept right on walking down. Nerve wrecking epilogue: The Bears continued to the left, the humans to the right, and a terrible tragedy was averted.

Kananaskis Country

Kananaskis Country or "K" Country, is comprised of large "in parts" spectacular wildlands located southwest of Calgary. It includes a cluster of many land ownership entities such as Provincial Park, Recreational Area, Wildlands, Provincial Forest, etc. It is bordered by highway 1 to the north, road 532 to the south, the British Columbia border to the west, and is due west of highway 22. Its land mass is over 100 kilometres long and 35 to 55 kilometres wide, approximately 4200 km². There are many enthusiasts who would like to see the day when the western half of it becomes a National Park as the scenery and environment undoubtedly warrant that. Some folks say that "K" Country should be connected to Waterton Park thereby creating a large new National Park which would provide continuous protected wildlands from the south to the far north. In 1858 when Captain John Palliser surveyed the area, he named two mountain passes and the river after a legendary native whose name was "Kineahkis (now Kananaskis).

Today the area is more a recreational playground for Calgarians and tourists than a park protecting the environment. Only the western part along the Continental Divide remains fairly pristine as access is limited. The rest of this fragmented land is overdeveloped. One of the main problems with "K" Country is its diverse legal status; every few kilometres or so, there is a different "Park". People get confused as to 'what is where'? Come hunting season "the bush war" often goes on where it should not!

"K" Country, being in the southern Rockies, is affected by warm Chinook winds and enjoys a milder climate allowing wildlife to flourish – all species are represented here except Caribou. Most raptors can be found here and fishing is good. Its proximity to Calgary makes "K" Country a great skiing destination with two large downhill ski areas and countless cross-country ski trails which attract thousands of sports enthusiasts. The Canmore Nordic Centre and Nakiska where the 1988 Winter Olympics were held are located in the Park. Please note that the major thoroughfare of the Park, highway 40, is closed from the lakes to Highwood House from December 1 to June 14 to allow a disturbance-free zone for wintering wildlife and spring calving.

The highest elevation in "K" Country is Mount Joffre (3450m) having on its north slopes Mangin Glacier; the second is massive Mount Sir Douglas (3406m) with large Haig Glacier on its southeast slopes.

Several large lakes like Spray, Barrier, and Upper and Lower Kananaskis, are all man-made and generate electricity. They are great recreational areas. A word of warning however – water levels and winds may change quickly spelling danger for boaters.

Highways are good and well-maintained year round. A gas station, a few hotels and lodges, a hostel, and restaurants, provide adequate service year round. Two guest ranches, a world-class golf course, and a large RV Park are all to be found here. So come and enjoy the activities of your choice but again bear in mind Bears – they are present and wild and some are hungry. It is a smart idea to treat any wilderness as if it was a National Park: do not disturb, move or remove anything, leave it pristine and wild. Take only pictures and leave gentle, soft footprints to ensure that Kananaskis will be there forever!

Right: The Three Sisters (2936m) overlook Canmore, Bow Valley and Spray Valley to the south. Not too long ago the Bow Valley here was wild, green, a place full of wildlife and natural beauty. Now it takes considerable effort to find undeveloped landscape in its natural state.

Above: *I*mmediately south of Spray Lakes along Smuts Creek some natural land still exists. The valley is flanked by the Kananaskis Range to the east and Spray Range on the west side. Meandering Smuts Creek features some small ponds or pits rich in minerals, combined with marshy boggy lands along the Creek – this is classic Moose country. During rutting season it is not unusual to spot five or more Moose in one place.

Left: *A*s colourful as it gets, autumn rewards us with mesmerizing hues. In the vicinity of Mt. Kidd lies the picturesque Wedge Pond recreational area. People come just to sit, enjoy the scenery, and breathe fresh clean air while enjoying a picnic. South of the pond looms The Wedge, a popular rock climbing site.

Above: Upper Kananaskis Lake area features diverse landscape and wildlife. A few hiking trails lead to genuine wilderness with campsites. Places like Three Isle Lake, Haig Glacier, Mt. Sir Douglas, Mt. Joffre, Mts. Sarrail and Foch, are not too distant.

Left: A quiet cozy cove at the east end of Upper Kananaskis Lake provides the view for this quaint early morning image. On the left stands imposing Mt. Foch (3180m) and on the right lofty Mt. Sarrail (3174m) looks on. Both can be climbed without much difficulty.

Above: The emerald green waters of lakes and rivers are predominant in glaciated areas. Upper Kananaskis Lake is no exception. The rock flour and silt of Haig and Mangin Glaciers and several other smaller ones cause that emerald colour. This image features the view to the west with pointy Mt. Putnik (2940m) on the left.

Left: Wedge Pond in all its morning glory! Photography features light, colour, shadows and shapes. Morning and late afternoon light provides most of these essential elements. As the saying goes "the early bird gets the worm", the photographer needs to be at a precise location before the sun comes up. Once in a while everything works well and a great photo is created.

Above: M*t. Black Prince (2932m) is adorned by the green healthy forest and gold autumn Larches of Spray Range, located six kilometers northwest of Upper Kananaskis Lake, as the crow flies. A relatively easy scramble from the southeast side, however the rock may be unstable and friable.*

Left: A*n extremely rugged and difficult climb, Opal Range is softened by a gentle autumnal foreground. On the left stands Mt. Brock (2902m); on the right looms Mt. Blane (2993m), first climbed in 1954 and 1955 respectively. Both are the water source of King Creek.*

Above: W*edge Pond is attractive year round, day or night. Here we witness a spectacular sunrise on Mt. Kidd (2958m) in late December; the large snowfall is yet to arrive. Kananaskis Country is a skier's paradise, both cross-country and downhill. The author spent a summer night on this summit (right) sleeping with a very obnoxious Pika.*

Left: F*rom Highwood Pass (2210m) climb a small peak to the south; from here a tremendous view unfolds westward toward Mt. Pocaterra (2934m), surrounded by gentle hills and lovely autumnal golden Larches. Grizzly Col nearby suggests that the area is Grizzly habitat – which it is!*

Banff National Park

Canada's first National Park - Banff – was created in 1885 to protect the newly discovered Sulphur Hot Springs which were envisioned as the potential site for a mountain resort – how right this vision turned out to be! The name 'Banff' is from Banffshire, Scotland, the birthplace of two financiers of the Canadian Pacific Railway. As the completed trans-continental railway in 1885 brought waves of curious visitors to this splendid new land, Banff started to grow and the Park was enlarged three times to attain today's size of 6641 km². UNESCO recognized this large and important ecosystem granting the Park World Heritage Site status.

Banff Park features many very attractive and unique land forms, rivers, lakes and endless mountains jutting skywards. Large icefields and glaciers can also be seen. The largest body of ice is the Wapta – Waputik Icefields System. Other lesser bodies of ice linger higher up, mostly on the north slopes of lofty mountains like: Bonnet, Forbes, Hector, Lyell, Temple, Victoria, and Willingdon, to name a few. Glacial silt-rock flour suspended in the water causes the emerald green colour of the lakes and rivers.

The Park is adorned by a few such first magnitude jewels as Lake Louise, Moraine Lake, Peyto Lake, Bow Lake, Waterfowl Lakes and the Bow River. As the global warming marches on and ice vanishes at alarming rates, these gorgeous emerald lakes will become history, turning into gray sloughs in the not too distant future. We can slow down the process or speed it up – it appears we cannot stop it because may people do not seem to care.

In the meantime great boreal forests cover deep lush valleys east of the Continental Divide providing a sustainable home environment to a variety of wildlife. The most common dweller is the majestic Elk, Mule and White Tail Deer. The mighty Moose once quite common seem to be on the decline in southern parts. The Park's northern perimeter sustains a small Caribou population. Sheep and Goat hold their own and can be seen on high craggy steep terrain.

Wherever there are numerous ungulates there are carnivores making a meal of them. Wolf, Coyote, Fox, Wolverine, Cougar, Lynx, and Bobcat all live here and are doing well. Most attractive of them all are the Bears, both Black and Grizzly, and they can be readily spotted especially in early summer and late autumn. The Grizzly spends summers in high alpine meadows while the Black Bear stays in the valley. Both are omnivorous, wild, potentially dangerous, and territorial. Do not despair if you see only one or two animals – there are a lot of them – and they well may be watching you from behind nearby bushes. You may have to come several times and the best sightings occur at twilight.

There are so many sights, hiking trails, and climbing routes in the Park but limited space does not permit us to mention them all. There are numerous publications available on them. Banff Park is a huge tourist attraction which draws circa four million visitors a year. Tourism and highway traffic is growing steadily and along with this growth comes extensive pressure and strain on the Park. Hundreds of animals are slaughtered by cars and trains every year and yet the idea of twinning and fencing of highways is progressing at a snail's pace. People are killed as well, but does anyone care?

Let's enjoy the Park in a rational sustainable manner – there is enough room for everyone as long as we are willing to play by the rules. Please remember that National Parks are meant to keep the wilderness unimpaired and pristine forever. Stay on the trails, do not move or take anything from the Park – it is not only against the law but logic as well. The Park will remain as long as we respect its purpose and status.

Right: **I**f you have not seen Mt. Victoria (3464m) and Lake Louise, you have not seen the Rockies. A quintessential place of pilgrimage for thousands of tourists year round. Come here ten times and see ten different moods and aesthetics of visual impressions. The mystery of a mountain sunrise!

Above: *A*long Icefields Parkway nestles spectacular glacial Bow Lake surrounded by a high world of rock and ice. To the south sprawls expansive Wapta Icefield and one of its glaciers – Bow Glacier – from which the Bow River originates. Bow Lake is known for its countless moods – here is one of them, a misty mysterious morning.

Left: *T*he monumental and sublime Mt. Temple (3543m) dominates the scene near Lake Louise. Its elevation ranks as eleventh highest in the Rockies. Many climbing routes lead to this popular summit, some comparatively easy, while others are extremely hazardous. Every two or three years someone lives have been lost here, mostly owing to avalanches or falls. First scaled in 1894, today there may be 25 people on the summit on any sunny weekend.

Showy pink Willow Herb line up by Mosquito Creek which is about to join the Bow River. This interesting mountain (circa 3000m) remains unnamed and is a northwest neighbour of Mt. Andromache along the Icefields Parkway (just north of Mosquito Campground and a Youth Hostel).

Pilot Mountain (2935m), first climbed in 1885, was always a prominent landmark guiding early travellers. The meadow is called Moose Meadow – indeed 20 years ago three or more Moose could be spotted here on a regular basis. Since then highway and railway traffic grew by approximately 150% and today most of the Moose are gone – killed off.

Above: A large cross-country ski race is held at Lake Louise on the first Sunday in March each year. Skiing in Canada, both Nordic and Alpine, is growing at a phenomenal rate. This is great news as winter sports are not only extremely enjoyable but healthy as well. Come March, wax your skis and join the fun!

Left: What is happening on solid frozen Lake Minnewanka in the dead of winter? Well, for some people it is not cold enough so they decide to cool it off. They are scuba divers who enjoy exploring murky depths of this deep Lake. In reality the water is not that much colder than it is in the summer.

Upper: *The majestic dweller of the Canadian Wilderness is the Moose Bull (Alces alces). Moose population is declining in direct proportion to the increase in development and human activities. Twenty years ago at Banff's Vermilion Lakes there were several Moose at any given time; today none remain.*

Lower: *Bow Summit at Icefields Parkway hosts a pretty stable Grizzly population. Early summer in Bear Society is party time, more technically called 'rutting' - when Bears get social. The remainder of the year Bears are somewhat solitary creatures. Photographing Grizzlies can be hazardous; this male staring at the author false charged twice.*

Left: *When the sky turns this dark, a storm is inevitable and it is time to head for cover. The author barely managed to reach the safety of his car when rain started to pour, soon changing to hail. Vermilion Lakes area, west of Banff.*

Above: The mesmerizing, illusive, Aurora Borealis or Northern Lights, is not a common sight to see or photograph at Banff Park. North of 60° latitude is the ideal place to view this amazing spectacle. The above photo was taken by Bath Creek west of Lake Louise. Aurora is an electric storm in the upper atmosphere and its characteristic movements depend on the intensity of the storm and solar winds. In the southern Polar region, the same phenomenon is known as Aurora Australis.

Left: Polaris or North Star is a nearly stationary star around which our celestial world circulates. Photographing Polaris is somewhat challenging; the moon causes a problem by casting too much light, rendering the stars very pale. On a moonless night exposure time must increase. Small invisible clouds, haze, or fog, can ruin the photo. This shot features Castle Mountain (2766m) with the trees being shaken by the wind with lighting from passing cars.

Above: $\mathcal{A}$n annual pilgrimage to Helen Lake at the end of July to enjoy and appreciate the beauty of the flowers; one year they are gorgeous and plentiful; next year hardly any to view. Temperature, moisture, and cycle, are the factors. Plants need a break every few years to rest, recuperate and continue the cycle. Helen Lake Trail is just east of Bow Lake on Icefields Parkway.

Left: "$\mathcal{R}$ush hour" at the passage between first and second Vermilion Lakes west of Banff. These three lakes feature an amazing diversity of wildlife from Elk to Beaver to Bald Eagle. One evening the author watched as a Grizzly approached from the highway underpass and chased some Elk cows with young calves. The Elk jumped into the water heading for an island pursued by the Grizzly. Darkness and distance obscured the event but most likely the Grizzly managed to get his dinner. Only 20% of young Deer survive.

Above and left: It is a matter of choice: pay $300 a night to stay in a prestigious hotel with every imaginable amenity, (Banff Springs Hotel) or, stay in a quinzee (a type of igloo) for the cost of an $8 camping permit (by Mt. Temple), with the only amenity being snow. Both are acceptable – the difference being a preference in lifestyle and perhaps....size of pocketbook!

Mt. Rundle (2998m) just southeast of Banff is a principal landmark in the Rockies that attracts thousands of visitors every year. This photograph presents Mount Rundle reflected in Second Vermilion Lake enhanced by a colourful sunset.

Another principal landmark, a guardian of the Bow Valley, is imposing Castle Mountain (2766m). It stands north of Castle Junction, mid-way between Banff and Lake Louise and is a major sightseeing, hiking and climbing site.

East of Lake Louise along the Bow River a railroad line winds its way through the lofty Rockies. To celebrate Canada Day an archaic steamer travels across the country bringing the nostalgia of bygone days. The photograph is taken at famous Morant's Curve which celebrates CPR's lifelong photographer.

Lower Waterfowl Lake is another emerald jewel among these unique glacial lakes of the Rockies. Except for a campground the area is pristine and verdant. There are four similar lakes in the immediate vicinity providing a real haven for the healthy young Moose population. Icy Howse Peak (3290m) looks down at Chephren Lake.

The great greenish-blue jewel of Banff Park – Peyto Lake – is visited year round by enchanted tourists who admire it from a low viewing platform. Here we offer a view from a much higher elevation giving the area a different perspective. The icy water emerges from Wapta Icefield and Peyto Glacier.

Lake Louise in the minds of many is that familiar postcard view with Mt. Victoria. On the left stands the less imposing and inconspicuous Fairview Mountain (2744m) but to be fair that mountain is interesting and beautiful and well worth the 'click'. Fairview Mountain is easily accessible by a good trail, taking approximately five hours round trip.

Above: Some like a warm luxurious hotel; others prefer cool winter camping. Wintry Chateau Lake Louise and Mt Richardson (3086m) catch the last hues of alpine glow; the ski area appears on the right – winter fun at its best! Lake Louise, and nearby Moraine Lake, offer great cross-country ski trails with abundant snow.

Left: There is never a shortage of brave dare-devils. Here in the upper part of Johnston Canyon a lone ice climber negotiates a vertical ice face. Today's equipment and climber skills make it look simple and safe. One significant hazard to be aware of here – the ice can separate from the rock and collapse, as this is March. It is preferable to climb it safely in January and February.

Above: Well hidden under the thick blanket of morning mist, Bow Lake rests by the foot of snowy Crowfoot Mountain (3050m). This is mid-October but winter seems to arrive early here. Bow Summit is the highest point of the Jasper Highway which means winter reigns here for at least seven months.

Left: Mt. Chephren or Black Pyramid (3266m) appears to be admiring its craggy eastern face reflected in Lower Waterfowl Lake. Indeed a serene peaceful morning image of a familiar landmark and major climbing site along Icefields Parkway. This is October and on a cold windless night ice will form and remain for a lengthy seven months.

A classic view of grand Moraine Lake. A short 12-kilometre drive from Lake Louise gets you to an unmatched paradise called The Valley of the Ten Peaks. There are more than ten peaks in the area, many glaciated and almost all exceeding 3000 metres in height. Endless possibilities of serious climbing, hiking (Grizzlies permitting), and canoeing exist here.

Above Moraine Lake a comfortable trail leads to the famous Larch Valley, where as the name implies, large stands of Larch trees turning yellow-gold in late September can be admired. Because the area is home to some aggressive Bears, park regulations require travel in groups of six or more for safety reasons. Mt. Fay (3234m) graces the horizon.

Above: *P*aradise Valley sprawls just south of Lake Louise and features natural attractions like Giant Steps, Lake Annette, Horseshoe Glacier, and high challenging mountains such as Mts. Temple, Hungabee and Lefroy. This autumnal photo portrays the rubble slopes of Mt. Temple, golden Larches, and on the right foreground the eastern slopes of Mt. Aberdeen (3151m).

Left: *A* distinctively impressive view unfolds from the summit of Ptarmigan Peak (3059m) looking north on a glorious mid-September morning. Only a small part of the glacier is visible in the foreground. The larger of the two Skoki Lakes is named Zigadanus, the smaller one is Myosotis. In the middle stands little Skoki Mountain (2697m); beyond that on the left is Little Pipestone Creek; on the right is the Red Deer River, followed by the Cyclone-Pipestone Mountains Group.

Kootenay National Park

This green pristine oasis is located west of the Continental Divide in the south central Rockies of British Columbia. Banff and Assiniboine Parks are to the east. The northern perimeter borders Yoho Park. To the west sprawl the Columbia Mountains. The Park is crossed by highway 93 only which was built in 1922 from Castle Junction at highway 1 to Radium Hot Springs and highway 95, a scenic 100 kilometre drive to enjoy. There is no railway, power lines or any development in this pure and verdant Park, which is as a National Park ought to be.

Two major crystal clear rivers drain the Park. In the north Vermilion River collects snow and icy waters and joins the south flowing Kootnenay River. A dozen large swift creeks abounding with life and beauty stretch across the Park. Situated west of the Continental Divide the area is blessed with sumptuous precipitation and often stormy summer weather, thus some devastating forest fires have occurred here in recent times. The Park was created in 1920 and is 1406 km² in size.

Nature was not very generous creating lakes here as only five small ones exist; Floe Lake being the largest is very attractive. The lush primordial forest, especially in the south, is breathtaking and impressive. Cedar trees in profusion can be admired. Tourist attractions? None, this is a National Park not an amusement park. Natural attractions? Many. In Radium, you can enjoy some time in the healthy and invigorating Radium Hot Springs pool. Nearby impressive Sinclair Canyon is seen, where iron-rich red rock attracts sheep and other mineral hungry animals. Sixteen kilometres further a roadside viewpoint offers a broad expanse of the Kootenay River Valley with endless forest and Mitchell and Vermilion Ranges to the north. At kilometer 63 along the scenic road, Vermilion Crossing offers information, food, lodging, and a picnic area – the Park's only services.

Ten kilometres further north, two interesting hiking trails are worth exploring: East – Hawk Creek to Ball Pass and west to Floe Lake, both amazingly beautiful and diverse, and each a full-day's hike. At kilometer 85 Paint Pots, mineral springs rich in iron bubble up in a few small pools, staining nearby Ochre Creek and Vermilion River with yellow-orange ochre. The next large natural attraction is three kilometres further north – Marble Canyon on Takumm Creek. A short deep canyon cut through hard polished limestone called marble which soon gives way upstream to wide-open Takumm Valley. A major hiking trail leads northwest to historic Fay Hut, recently rebuilt after being destroyed in a forest fire in 2003. The trail continues on to picturesque Kaufmann Lake and Opabin Pass leading into Yoho's Lake O'Hara area.

Nearby on the east side an easy trail leads to Stanley Glacier lookout through a new regrowth of a forest which was destroyed by a 1968 fire. Seven kilometres up the road Vermilion Pass is accessed; from here the water flows west to the Pacific and east to the Atlantic Ocean. A short distance away is the boundary of Banff National Park.

In recently-burned areas the trails may be closed or restricted due to danger of falling trees – to be safe enquire before proceeding. Wherever it is safe to enter, go and have a peek, see what nature's fertilizer – ash - has done. You will be greeted with a massive carpet of flowers and plant life – amazing beauty! This is the real, natural and great Kootenay National Park.

Right: The Vermilion River is born at Vermilion Pass (1651m) by the Banff/Kootenay Parks border where nearby Storm Mountain and Mt. Whymper are the first water suppliers. Upper-northern parts of the Park are abundant with glaciers and permanent snowfields providing plenty of melt water. Vermilion River joins Kootenay River in the southern part of the Park. The pinkish flowers along the fertile river flats are broad-leafed Willow Herb (Epilobium latifolium), a close relative of Fireweed.

The south-central part of the Park is flanked on the east by 'impenetrable' Mitchell Range (photo). The dense forest and large river effectively stop any exploration or intrusion. The only major trail north of here, the Simpson River trail circa 25 kilometres long, allows access to Mount Assiniboine Park.

The Vermilion River meanders through a narrow valley of steep green slopes where rain and snow precipitation is generous. These lush verdant slopes are home to Grizzly Bears during summer, providing them with gourmet meals consisting of new tender shoots of a variety of plants.

Above: J*ust north of Vermilion Crossing a small pond provides this splendid reflection of the Vermilion Range at sunrise. The pointy-conical peak on the left is Mt. White Tail (2970m), the centre one at an elevation of 3065m is unnamed, while on the right is Mt. Verendrye (3086m). Access to this group is by Verendrye Creek trail by Vermilion Crossing.*

Left: A *major fire in 2003 destroyed a large part of northern Kootenay Park. Here near Marble Canyon two years later the forest floor is alive and lush, but these burned tree trunks have yet to fall down. Walking here on a windy day is extremely hazardous and not advised. Access to burned and rebuilt Fay Hut is closed until falling trees are removed (inquire before proceeding).*

As Kootenay Park receives adequate moisture, vegetation flourishes everywhere. Gorgeous flowers are abundant throughout the summer in lower valley and high alpine meadows. If you wish to experience a colourful, aromatic paradise, visit Floe Lake near the end of July and then again at the end of September to view the golden Larches.

Upper: Wild Rose (Rosa woodsii); lower: Indian Paintbrush (Castilleja miniata); on the left a carpet of flowers on a small clearing created by the recent fire.

Yoho National Park

Yoho National Park is comparatively small in size but very large in beauty and land features. It is located west of the Continental Divide and Kicking Horse Pass along the Trans-Canada Highway. Its beginning goes back to 1886, one year after Banff Park was created. The Park protects 1313 km^2 of spectacular landscape – no wonder the native Cree called this place 'awe and wonder inspiring'.

The Park is sliced in half by the highway and railway, along which most facilities are located. East of the railway town of Field, B.C., completed in 1909, a world engineering wonder, the spiral tunnels are located. One can watch for hours as a train disappears into the mountain, reappears in another place, only to disappear again into yet another tunnel. The Park hosts more than two dozen lofty peaks over 3000 metres high. Yoho shares two large icefields with Banff – Wapta and Waputik – and at least five smaller bodies of ice. The prime natural wonder in Yoho Valley is 300-metre high Takakkaw Falls which means 'splendid ' in native language, and it is indeed splendid. The melt water comes from Waputik Icefield and Daly Glacier to the east. The Takakkaw road is closed for the winter at first snowfall. Nearby in upper Yoho Valley, remnants of fast melting Yoho Glacier can be seen after a lengthy strenuous hike and scramble. Not that long ago the Glacier was visible from the end of the trail viewpoint. At the northwest end of the Valley once mighty Twin Falls is fast becoming 'Unifalls' as one falls grows larger at the expense of the other which almost disappears.

Continuing west past Field, an 11 kilometre side road open year round leads to the jewel of the Park – Emerald Lake. The scenery is unsurpassed, nature is verdant, mountains reach the sky, and the Lake lives up to its name. Take a canoe and share the Lake with Loons. East of Wapta Lake, south of the highway, a restricted road not for the public, leads 11 kilometres south to another jewel, Lake O'Hara. This most attractive area visited by thousands in the past has incurred serious environmental degradation. There is now a quota system in effect restricting visiting. The area is blessed with a few more wonders like Lake McArthur, Lake Oesa, as well as a few smaller ones. A vibrant Grizzly community nearby keeps several trails permanently closed. A commercial lodge, an alpine hut, and a campground provide accommodation. Lofty peaks exceeding 3350m/11,000 ft. can be viewed.

Further west along the highway, Ottertail River trail allows exploring deep into the Ottertail Range area with mighty Mount Goodsir (3562m) the ninth elevation in the Rockies. Further to the south the Hoodoo Creek is worth exploring; watch for diverse wildlife as lofty and icy Mount Vaux (3319m) and Chancellor Peak (3280m) dominate the scenery.

Near the southwest end of the Park, Wapta Falls on the Kicking Horse River is a "must see" feature. The first half of July is the best time to visit as early summer runoff make the falls roar. Being under the warmer moist Pacific air influence, the Park supports rare trees like Cedar, Western Maple, and Mountain Ash, allowing for a lush and green environment. The onus is on each of us to keep the Park healthy and beautiful.

Right: World famous Emerald Lake, a sparkling jewel of the Rockies, features the gentle grandeur of this high mountain environment. The Lake is surrounded by impressive mountains such as The President, Wapta, and Mt. Burgess (2599m). A paradise for hikers, climbers, canoeists, bird watchers, and photographers.

Above: $\mathcal{S}$outhwest of Lake O'Hara stands monumental Odaray Mountain (3159m), not a hike but a pleasant scramble, until one gets close to the summit on the southeast ridge. The crest is broken by two chimneys which can cause serious difficulties. To the right is Cathedral Mountain (3189m), an equally challenging climb.

Left: $\mathcal{H}$ere a tale of nature at work unfolds as Twin Falls takes their turns. Not long ago the Falls on the left was larger but now it simply seems to disappear. Water carves the rock on the right Falls faster and if this process continues, the left Falls will soon receive water only during spring runoff.

Impressive and lofty Mt. Vaux (3319m) reflected in marshes west of Ottertail Range. Why are the trees red? Mountain Pine Beetles have invaded the forest, killing trees in huge numbers. Park personnel attempt prescribed fires to contain this pest, seldom with adequate success. Good or bad, nature has its ways! A new healthy forest will always emerge on a dead forest site.

*J*ust west of Kicking Horse Pass (1625m) and Wapta Lake, a small flowery meadow flourishes in early August. Showy Fireweed is at home and doing well in most of these locations. The mountain in the background is the eastern arm of Cathedral Mountain massif and on the right edge a tiny bit of Mt. Stephen is visible.

Above and left: When looking at the splendour of Takakkaw Falls people ask – where is all that water coming from? The panoramic photo above has some answers. Large Waputik Icefield and Daly Glacier located between ice-clad Mt. Balfour (3272m), on far left, and Mt. Daly (3152m) on far right (not visible) provide the melt water. Takakkaw Falls is most impressive in late June and July when snow and ice melt profusely. On the left is a more detailed close-up of this unique phenomenon. These are not aerial photos; the author is an avid mountain climber.

Mt. Field (2635m) does not much resemble Mt. Everest. A trail hike from Field or Emerald Lake gets access to Burgess Pass (2182m) from where a short steep scramble rewards you with interesting panoramic views. Most impressive of all, the imposing rugged north face of Mt. Stephen is just a stone's throw away to the south. The nasty southern ridge of Wapta Mountain (2778m) looms above the tent.

On the summit of Mt. Field (2635m) enjoying nocturnal sightseeing. How to reach there is described on the opposite page. This ten-minute exposure photo features on the far left horizon Mt. Goodsir and white Mt. Vaux of the Ottertail Range. The meandering Kicking Horse River and the town of Field are seen along the well-lit Trans-Canada Highway. One leg of the tripod rested on solid rock one inch away from a sheer 1400 metre vertical drop. The phrase 'living dangerously' came to mind.

In the western part of the Rockies along the Kicking Horse River a railway line winds along the narrow verdant valley. This is the world famous Rocky Mountaineer Rail Tours train travelling from Calgary and Jasper to Vancouver – a once-in-a-lifetime, unforgettable trip providing the best in luxurious travel.

South of Lake O'Hara is easily accessible Mt. Schaffer (2692m), from where this high alpine world is viewed. On the left skyline is Mt. Huber (3368m), the snowy icy peak at the centre is imposing Mt. Lefroy (3423m), and the middle ground graces Yukness Mountain (2847m). A keen eye will notice on the left a small sliver of Mary Lake, Lake O'Hara and Oesa.

Jasper National Park

The pride of all Rocky Mountain National Parks – Jasper Park – is a true champion in many ways. It is 1000 km² larger than Banff, Kootenay, Waterton and Yoho Parks combined and is all wild and green. The small town of Jasper located in the centre of the Park is the service hub for tourists and is the seat of the Parks Administration. Originating at Lake Louise – Icefields Parkway – highway 93 built in 1940 and improved in 1950, is rightly called the world's most scenic mountain road. The Park is crossed from east to west by a major transportation corridor including highway 16 and the railway from Edmonton to the Pacific Coast. Although not pretty features, the latter are necessary as is the Trans-Canada Highway through Banff National Park.

Jasper Park established in 1907 encompasses 10,878 km², about the size of Jamaica. Several grand natural attractions unmatched anywhere grace the Park. To the south at the Banff Park boundary, known the world over, is the Columbia Icefield which sprawls on nearly 200 km². From that high icy plateau descend several large rivers of tumbling ice called glaciers, some as long as eight kilometres. The Columbia Icefield is home to numerous lofty challenging mountains, the dominant one being Mount Columbia (3747m), the second highest elevation of the Rockies.

Moving northwest along Sunwapta and Athabasca Rivers, many lofty mountains can be seen on both sides of the valley. Only 30 kilometres from Jasper, Athabasca Falls, a major cataract plunges deep into a dark gorge.

A short six kilometres from Jasper a winding road brings us to the foot of glaciated Mount Edith Cavell (3363m) a major, serious climbing site. From here the spectacular Tonquin Valley and Amethyst Lakes can be accessed in one long day, or stay a few days in a campground, alpine hut, or two commercial outlets. A virtual paradise to be sure! Just north of Jasper a number of scenic lakes are accessible by a fine network of hiking trails. Southeast of Jasper other prime Park attractions, namely Medicine and Maligne Lakes, are reachable by an all-weather road. A 48 kilometre drive will reward you with the most spectacular scenery around – 22 kilometre long emerald Maligne Lake is surrounded by high ice-clad mountains and endless pure unspoiled wilderness. Wildlife here is numerous and diverse. The mighty Moose is at home in the marshy meadows, Grizzlies roam the high valleys, and Mountain Caribou can be spotted as well. Wolf packs roam between the lakes in search of their next meal. Of course, expectancy to see all these animals at one time is unrealistic. They are present but perhaps hidden behind bushes nearby. It may take several trips, mostly at twilight, for these sightings.

Along highway 16 east are numerous lakes and marshes but in reality the area is rather dry due to strong westerly winds. Still Moose, Elk, Sheep, and Goat, are common here. Just before reaching the east Park gate, the remains of the Pocahontas Coal Mine can be explored. To the south in Fiddle Valley is situated Miette Hotsprings surrounded by mountains, the hottest springs in the Rockies with temperatures reaching 54°C.

West of Jasper the landscape changes as the Continental Divide gets much more precipitation than the east side, thus nature is lusher. Further west in Mount Robson Park, the monarch of the Rockies, mighty Mt. Robson (3954m) waits to be admired.

The northwest part of Jasper Park, three times the size of Yoho Park, is total wilderness. There are only a few hiking trails that penetrate deeply and only experienced hardy souls need apply because you are totally on your own - 70 or 90 kilometres from anywhere, with only Grizzly and Wolves for company. North of Jasper Park sprawls huge Willmore Wilderness Park – a wild paradise, untouched by the bulldozer civilization, thank God!

Right: The quintessential landmark of Jasper Park, the glorious Spirit Island on pristine Maligne Lake, meets all the criteria of a super tourist sight. The only way to get here is by boat or canoe; no hiking trails exist for accessing. Why? To preserve and protect this spectacular and undisturbed wilderness.

Above. This rainbow can be compared to the Aurora Borealis – it appeared from nowhere, lingered for a while and quickly disappeared. What causes or creates a rainbow? Rainbows occur when rain falls opposite to the sunlight, most frequently in the morning or late afternoon. The basic colours of the rainbow are red, orange, yellow, green, blue, indigo and violet. One rainbow may contain all these colours, while another only some of the colours, depending on light and rain intensity. The photo is taken southeast of Jasper.

Left: A short drive north of Jasper leads to Pyramid Lake in the shadow of Pyramid Mountain (2766m). Early morning light reveals all the craggy features of its southeast face. For those with boundless energy, climbing this mountain is not a huge task. The 12 kilometre access road may present some drudgery but the actual climb over stable quartzite blocks is a pleasant scramble. Mt. Robson is clearly visible on the western horizon.

The middle part of Tangle Falls captured on film on a moody overcast morning. Tangle Creek and its subsidiaries drain a large area to the north and east including Tangle Ridge which is snowbound until late summer. The ideal time to view the Falls is early summer when the water is high and roaring.

*T*here are not many areas in the Rockies where one can drive a car to the toe of a glacier. One such location is Athabasca Glacier and another is Mt. Edith Cavell (3363m). A narrow winding road gets you there, and then a short trail leads to Cavell and Angel Glaciers on the formidable north wall of Mt. Edith Cavell. People have been injured here by falling ice so keep a safe distance. Mt. Edith Cavell reflects its white face in Cavell Lake.

Above: M*aligne Lake is a sight to behold. So many moods, features and angles, greet you when you look at this blue beauty. The Lake can be reached by a scenic road open year-round, 48 kilometres southeast of Jasper. Regardless of the high altitude and northern latitude, wildlife abound here. Moose, Deer, Grizzly and Wolf thrive. The dominant mountain is a massif of Mt. Charlton (3217m) on the left and Mt. Unwin (3268m).*

Left: I*n the south-central part of the Park along the Endless Chain Range nestles picturesque Honeymoon Lake, a pretty serene place with a small campground, ideal for a brief relaxing getaway from it all. In any direction stretches spectacular wilderness surrounded by endless forests and majestic mountains. From a roadside pullover just west of here, Mt. Columbia (3747m) is visible to the south.*

A large river like the Athabasca is a major barrier, holding wildlife on one side for a long time. Animals however have social, economic and safety reasons for crossing the water. High water poses danger of drowning – during freeze up and spring thaw countless animals drown. Animals cannot estimate the thickness of the ice – as is the case with some skidooers! Here we see two Elk crossing the Athabasca River near Jasper as Mt. Edith Cavell looks on.

When bivouacking on a mountain, one's gear often becomes soggy or just plain wet. If the next day is full of sunshine and warmth, all will dry quickly. If, however, the day is rainy, then mountaineering is not much fun. Here on a sunny morning, the author dries his 'stuff' on the lower slopes of Mt. Clitheroe (2749m) in front of the fascinating The Ramparts and Amethyst Lakes in the Tonquin Valley, nearly a 40 kilometre gorgeous round trip.

Above: To construct an igloo you do not require a bank loan, only a shovel and two hours of strenuous work. An igloo is warmer and quieter than a tent and it feels like you really belong to the land. Of course, not all igloos are created equal; the author being an artist knows how to build one in style. It is late winter by Mt. Athabasca (3499m) on the left, and Mt. Andromeda (3444m). Life is good!

Left: After another two hours of exhausting scramble you arrive at the peak (2790m) north of Opal Hills and Maligne Lake. Looking to the west endless peaks of Queen Elizabeth and Colin Ranges sweep the horizon. Above the climber Opal Peak rises sharply, dusted by the first autumn snow. It is an exhilarating feeling to be alive on top of a mountain – give it a try. In the hidden valley to the west one may spot a Grizzly or Caribou.

No, this is not an Irish countryside – but we do have in the Rockies a three-leafed plant called 'clover'. Quite common throughout North America a Mourning Cloak butterfly rests on these nutrients-rich plants. The butterfly plays an important role in the cross-pollination of many flowering plants.

Wild Rose (Rosa woodsii) a prickly shrub can reach 1.5 metres in height with a delicate five-petal flower in the wild state – a garden variety rose may have more petals. This plant of genus Rosa, Family Rosaceae, can range in colour from pale pink to almost crimson red. Its appearance and fragrance is mesmerizing.

Maligne Lake can be accessed by a scenic road 48 kilometres southeast of Jasper. Winter lingers here for about seven months because of the high altitude (1690m), while the town of Jasper (elevation 1063m) enjoys a much shorter winter. The ice at the Lake's outlet melts first allowing newly-arrived waterfowl to cool off and find food after a long flight from the warm south.

Mt. Kerkeslin (2956m) dominates the Athabasca Valley near Athabasca Falls. No hiking or scrambling here; this is strictly a climbing site. Appropriately the mountain is year-round home to a large colony of sure-footed fearless Mountain Goats which often wander down to river cliffs rich in minerals. The photo depicts the west face; north slopes are entirely covered by a large body of crevassed ice.

If Eskimo or Inuit people could live in igloos for thousands of years, we too can for a night or two. Maligne Lake bathed in full moonlight provides a very romantic night setting with a difference, for mountain lovers. Also see caption on page 93.

Another romantic setting in the great outdoors by the Sunwapta River just northwest of Columbia Icefield. Spring is around the corner and shortly runoff water will fill the valley. A sharp-eyed Warden passing by did not feel that romantic when he ordered us to be 'out of here' in a half hour.

Upper: M*ajestic Bighorn Sheep (Ovis canadensis) are still quite common in the Rockies. Not hunted in National Parks, they lost their fear of man and often beg for handouts along the roadways. Please do not feed wildlife; it is not only illegal but also contributes to many road kills.*

Lower: A *fearless, sure-footed mountain climber - the Mountain Goat (Oreamnos americanus), lives up to its reputation. It climbs nearly vertical walls where alpine vegetation thrives on narrow ledges. The Goat is confined to steeps for safety as on flats it is vulnerable.*

Upper: The monarch of all ungulates, the Moose (Alces alces), is the world's largest deer - a browser which also feeds on aquatic vegetation. An adult cow may weigh up to 550 kilograms, while a bull may exceed 750 kilograms. A Moose's appetite is prodigious – a cow may consume as much as 25 kilograms of food per day.

Lower: The Elk (Cervus canadensis) is one of the most popular and most often seen dweller of the Rockies. Elk spend the summer on higher ground descending into lower valleys for late autumn and winter. During rutting season, the bulls often fight bloody battles for dominance over large herds of cows.

Above: This is in the vicinity of the Columbia Icefield where even on the warmest summer day the air is cool at best. It makes one wonder how these hardy Fireweed flowers manage to survive here at all. Left to right: Lofty Mt. Athabasca (3490m) is the eastern sentinel of the Icefield; icy Mt. Andromeda (3444m) is quite challenging. Next is what remains of the rapidly receding Athabasca Glacier.

Left: By the Columbia Icefield along Icefields Parkway the landscape is somewhat inhospitable and bleak comprising rock, gravel, silty moraines, and not much else. Regardless, here and there, large clusters of flowers manage to cling to this cold, harsh reality. To the west of Mt. Athabasca (3490m) on sheltered flats along the Sunwapta River, a great colony of Willow Herb (Epilobium latifolium) finds a suitable habitat.

Mount Robson Provincial Park

Home of Mount Robson (3954m/12972ft), the lofty monarch of the Rockies, Mount Robson Provincial Park protects a large wilderness just west of Jasper National Park. The Fraser River, the Park's major drainage, begins near Fraser Pass and flows west to Moose Lake towards Mount Robson, then to the Pacific Ocean 1370 kilometres away. The Fraser River is named for a fur trader Simon Fraser who in 1808 travelled the river by canoe and on foot to the Ocean. Established in 1913 the Park encompasses 2248 km² of original untouched impenetrable wilderness, especially on the south side, as the Fraser River and a dense "rain forest" prevent any intrusions.

Highway 16 and the railway cross the Park via very low Yellowhead Pass (1131m). Nearby Yellowhead Lake and Mountain (2458m) are interesting sights and on the south side a trail to Mt. Fitzwilliam (2907m) is worth exploring.

Four kilometres east of Moose Lake along Moose River an incredible wilderness trail heads north towards Moose Pass (2002m) nearly a 50 kilometre trek, then proceeds west along the source of Smoky River – Adolphus Lake – and Robson Pass to Berg Lake, Kinney Lake, and back to highway 16 at Robson Village, another 35 kilometres. This over 80 kilometre, six-day trek through totally wild remote terrain is an adventure unmatched anywhere. Only a party of several experienced and well-equipped campers should attempt it and be prepared for any eventuality. Coincidentally, this was also the route that the first Mount Robson explorers used in the early days without the trail's benefit.

Mount Robson is a major destination for climbers from around the world. There is no easy way up this mighty summit. Exploration commenced in 1908, several attempts were made mostly from the southeast via Robson Glacier, and The Dome (3078m) was attained. Another attempt was made via the northwest side and the Kinney-Phillips team almost made it to the summit in dangerous weather conditions – but it was not the summit. The breakthrough came in 1913 when Albert McCarthy and William Foster guided by Conrad Kain climbed from Robson Glacier, The Dome, southeast icy terraces – cutting hundreds of steps - and set foot on the mighty summit for the first time. In intervening years many attempts were made via various routes, most to no avail. Even today not many parties reach the summit due to unpredictable weather and dangerous snow-ice conditions.

Between Kinney and Berg Lakes is the Valley of a Thousand Falls (make it ten). Emperor Falls is truly impressive as mighty Whitehorn Mountain (3395m) looks on silently from the west. By Robson Village, Overlander Falls on the Fraser River is worth seeing, and west of the Park's boundary Rearguard Falls is the major barrier for migrating Chinook Salmon. Only a few make it up the Falls to be stopped by higher Overlander Falls. Near the very southwest tip of the Park stands Mount Terry Fox named to commemorate the heroic across-Canada run by one-legged cancer victim, Terry Fox, to raise money for cancer research.

Robson Park has got it all – fabulous scenery, rich wildlife, beautiful green pristine wildlands – what more could one ask? Just enjoy, admire and preserve the Park for future generations.

Right: The monarch of the Canadian Rockies – Mt. Robson (3954m) – as seen on an early splendid October morning. There are certain months when the weather allows only ten days to actually see the monarch; the remainder of the time solid clouds drape his majesty's crown. When moist Pacific air meets dry cool northern air and the high wall of the Continental Divide, the result is mostly rain or snow.

Above: Overlander Falls on the Fraser River is circa ten metres high, but the sheer volume of water effectively stops the Chinook Salmon migration to spawn. Sometime ago the author witnessed and photographed a kayaker going over the Falls. The kayak hit the whirlpool's bottom and became stuck. It took that young dare-devil 62 seconds to undo the harness and free himself; a close call to be sure!

Left: The impressive refined beauty of the north side of Mt. Robson (3954m) and Berg Lake as seen from a high north ridge. On the left shines Berg Glacier and above it towers The Helmet (3401m). In the centre is the hair-raising north face and Misty Glacier below it; on the right notoriously treacherous Emperor Ridge. Robson Glacier east of here provides most of the water for Berg Lake, which is the icy beginning of the Robson River.

Upper: M*t. Fitzwilliam (2907m) is a dominant mountain around Yellowhead Pass in the eastern section of the Park. A hiking trail leads south allowing exploration of several lakes and mountains in the vicinity.*

Lower: A *tourist view of Mt. Robson (3954m) photographed in late September on a rare cloudless and calm day. Milder climate west of the Continental Divide allows rare trees such as cedar, ash, and even a linden tree to thrive.*

Upper: *According to the poet: 'flowers blossom everywhere for those who want to see them'. At Robson Park flora is rich and plentiful indeed for anyone to see and smell all summer long.*

Lower: *Several kilometers long, a multi-peaked ridge like Yellowhead Mountain (2412m) is located just north of Yellowhead Lake, 33 kilometres west of Jasper. North of the mountain a totally pristine wilderness sprawls along Miette River.*

Above: M̃oose Lake is 13 kilometres long and the Fraser River flows right through it. Flanked by gentle mountains - on the left is Emerald Ridge of the Selwyn Range and Rainbow Range is on the right. By the south shore, two kilometers up the slope roars large Thunder Falls accessible only by boat; the forest here is very dense.

Left: D̃o you feel the power of the mountain? In the case of Mt. Robson (3954m), you do. The size of the monarch is enormous and overwhelming, stretching nearly ten kilometers across with an elevation difference from the base to the summit of almost three kilometers, twice the size of the average mountain in the Rockies. Mt. Robson is climbed by very few parties each year due to its monumental size, unpredictable weather and snow-ice conditions.

The Author

From a young age, George gravitated in right directions. Strong discipline, demanding parents and school, combined for a trouble-free youth. Scouting was very instrumental in opening up the great outdoors, mountaineering and skiing, in his early years. Enthusiasm, setting goals, and hard work always pay off.

George has climbed over 400 mountains and explored most of the wild lands of western North America. He is a world traveler, having visited 37 countries to date. He published the first book on the Canadian Rockies in 1978.

George's books sell at slightly above cost making them readily available to everyone. His main aim is to promote the sport of mountaineering, a healthy lifestyle, and the Rockies' refined and extraordinary beauty. Producing enough quality photos in one year to enable him to publish one or two books is not an easy task due to notoriously capricious mountain weather, but with his persistence and hard work George manages to get it done.

This volume, his 39th book, makes him Canada's most productive pictorial book author. Our research shows that no one author has published as many books about mountains anywhere. For this reason, we presume that this makes George the world's most prolific author in the mountain pictorial book category. Not bad for an unpretentious, modest man, who just loves to explore the mountains, rain or shine. George does not seek publicity through the news media or boast about his activities. Publicity, fame and money, are not his goals, being totally non-materialistic. Instead his wealth is deeply enshrined in his heart and soul. With his innumerable rich experiences on high silvery ridges and lofty summits, he is a wealthy man who does not require security to guard his wealth.

Mountain photography is an arduous, demanding, often dangerous, line of work. Sudden changes in weather, snow, and extreme drops in temperature, can leave one stranded on top of a difficult mountain for long periods of time; if unprepared, one may perish due to cold. At lower elevations, avalanches or Bears, can pose serious danger. In spite of all these factors, George refuses to slow down or become complacent about his work. He continues to climb and photograph his beloved Rockies as he has done for the last 36 years.

The author would like to say a few words to young people, who at ages 16 or 17, are wide-eyed and just approaching the crossroads of their life. "Be aware that a single unguarded turn can take you down a dangerous path: smoking, drinking, drugs, and crime - a life destroyed. There is another direction, however, that can take you to pursue education, an interesting profession, a healthy lifestyle, and success." The author realizes that for some young people, it does not always seem "cool" to do the right thing, it's boring! "Do you prefer jail? Take the right turn!" Books are always influential and the author hopes that his life's work which has helped two generations of eager young Canadians reach a healthy summit in their lives will continue to be of interest to young people everywhere. Mountaineering is healthy, it builds character, instills strong stamina, and it certainly offers more than any noisy smoky pub. So how about climbing a mountain!

While the author/publisher encourages the exploring of mountains, he also warns of the dangers and hazards which exist there, even in places where one would never expect any problems. This book is not intended to be a climbing guide but some of the contents may induce interest in climbing and prompt a visit to the mountains. Do it at your own risk, we disclaim any liability for your actions. We repeat - exploring and climbing involves serious risk and danger. Before undertaking any such activity, it is strongly advised that you take a mountaineering course, join a club or travel with experienced parties, never solo. Be diligent, play it wisely and safely, and enjoy the great Canadian Rockies.

This book was created in Alberta by Albertans
Printed in Singapore by CS Graphics
Text Editor: Helen Turgeon
Design: George Brybycin
Typeseting: K & H United Co.
First Edition: 2006

This is George Brybycin's 39th book.
Front cover: Mt. Robson
Back cover: Mt. Assiniboine
GB PUBLISHING, Box 6292, Station D,
Calgary, Alberta Canada T2P 2C9

George Brybycin's collection of 20,000 35mm colour slides is
FOR SALE at nominal price.
Offers may be tendered to GB Publishing at the address above.

ISBN 0-919029-40-X